CUSTODY
by Tom Wainwright

TEAM
ANGELICA

Published April 2017 by Team Angelica Publishing,
an imprint of Angelica Entertainments Ltd

Team Angelica Publishing
51 Coningham Road
London W12 8BS

www.teamangelica.com

A CIP catalogue record for this book is available from the British Library

ISBN 978-0-9955162-1-2

Printed and bound by Lightning Source

Credits:

Created by Urbain Hayo aka Urban Wolf
Written by Tom Wainwright
Directed by Gbemisola Ikumelo

Cast:

BROTHER – Urbain Hayo
SISTER – Kiké Brimah
MOTHER – Karlina Grace-Paṣeda
LOVER – Sacharissa Claxton

Movement Director: Cindy Claes
Designer: Phil Newman
Composer: Dan Bilbrough aka Sekrit
Sound Designer/Production Manager: Michael Francis
Lighting Designer: John Castle
Dramaturge: John R Gordon
Assistant Director: Eddie Howell
Producer: Hannah Tookey

Presented by Ovalhouse and Art Machine in collaboration
with FAITH Drama Productions

Creator

Urbain Hayo, also known as the performer Urban Wolf, is artistic director of The Art Machine. He has primarily worked as an actor in the theatre, but has also ventured into writing, producing and performance art. His work focuses on telling stories that challenge and change society. *Custody* is Urbain's first produced play. He was moved to create it after watching the documentary film *Injustice*.

Playwright

Tom Wainwright is a writer and performer based in Bristol. Credits include *The Wainwrights* and *The Strange Vanishing of Julian Quark* (BBC Radio 4), *Noisy Nativity* (Tobacco Factory), *I Am The Walrus* (Young Vic); *Banksy: The Room In The Elephant* (Oran Mor/Tobacco Factory/Arcola Theatre); *Altogether Now* (North Wall), *Barry The Beaver* (MAYK), *Buttercup* (Bristol Ferment, touring), *This Is Only A Test* (Box of Tricks Theatre), *Pedestrian* (Theatre Bristol/Bristol Old Vic/Seared Productions), *Muscle* (Hull Truck/Bristol Old Vic, published by Oberon Books), *Emo* (ATC/Bristol Old Vic Young Company), *Hansel and Gretel* and *10W2* (Theatre Royal Bath, The Egg), *Run and Fallen* (Bristol Old Vic Young Company) and *Come to Where I'm From* (Paines Plough), *One*, *Love in Idleness*, *The Grill Chef* and Christmas sketch-show *Jesus Christ it's Christmas* (Bristol Old Vic/Paper Aeroplane). Tom has worked as an actor for Bristol Old Vic, Tobacco Factory, Theatre Royal Bath, Theatre Alibi, Scamp Theatre, Myrtle Theatre, Bodies in Flight, BBC1, Radio 4 and performed with street show *The Big Heads*.

Tom says: 'It is a total honour to have been part of this project. The warmth, compassion, humour and courage of the families we have met and spoken to as we've created this show has been truly inspiring. This play is dedicated to them and to anyone who has lost a loved one in police custody.'

Director

Gbemisola Ikumelo is a writer/director and actress. She founded FAITH Drama Productions in 2005 and is the current Artistic Director. In this role she has directed *Life On The Stairs* (UK tour), *The Fiddler* (Unicorn Theatre), *Next Door* (Cockpit Theatre), *The Den* (site-specific) and *But I don't like girls* (Pleasance Theatre). As a freelancer she has also directed *Spring* (Riverside Studios) and Yvonne Dodoo's *Liquid Gold* at the Almeida Theatre (Tiata Delights Festival) In 2011 she was awarded a John Fernald award for young directors. In 2015 her debut film *ONEWAY* won a Best UK Short at the UK Christian Film Festival. Other short films include *The Judge, Brass Balls* and *Keep It Together.*

As an actress Gbemisola has won a Carleton Hobbs Award which has led to working as part of BBC's Radio Drama company, and many years of appearing in well over 30 radio plays since; and has played alongside Sally Phillips in the BBC's *Clare in the Community.* Other acting credits include; Shenzi in West-End and UK tour of *The Lion King*, Crystal in Salisbury Playhouse's *Little Shop Of Horrors*, Mickey in Manchester Royal Exchange's *The Night Watch*, WPC Stewart in *Broadchurch*, Kadean in BBC sitcom *Sunny D* and Chinasa Obi in Arcola Theatre's *New Nigerians.*

Gbemisola says: 'FAITH Drama Productions is an award-winning non-profit arts organisation producing bold work locally and nationally. We are BAME led, and our performance work focuses on new writing, producing theatre and film, and staging combined arts productions that are topical and aimed at diverse audiences and communities. We also provide professional training and development programmes for the benefit of emerging and professional creatives through courses, workshops and internship opportunities.

We believe the arts have a role to play in healing broken communities, giving the oppressed a voice, and we do this by responding with compassion, love and the truth! To that end, much of our creative work travels into unconventional spaces to reach wider communities, and we spend much time building up and nurturing people – diamonds in the rough who have something important to say at a time such as this. Urbain Hayo, creator of *Custody*, was one of those people and we are proud to have spent many years supporting him as an emerging artist. This play is a testament to the power of the diamond in the rough!'

Dramaturge

John R Gordon is an award-winning novelist, playwright and screenwriter of black gay lives. He worked on the groundbreaking US-based TV series *Noah's Arc*, wrote the autobiography of porn-star Bobby Blake, and his screenplay for *Noah's Arc: Jumping the Broom* earned him an NAACP Image Award nomination. He is the creator of HIV-themed graphic novella *Yemi & Femi's Fun Night Out*. With Rikki Beadle-Blair he is the founder of outsider imprint Team Angelica Publishing. His sixth novel, *Souljah*, was nominated for a Lambda Best Novel award, and he is currently revising his seventh, *Drapetomania*, a tale of same-gender love set in slavery times in the American South.

*

Designer

Phil Newman is a freelance set and costume designer whose recent credits include: *A Christmas Carol* (Little Theatre by the Park, Chesham), *Jungle Book* & *High School Musical* (Elgiva Theatre, Chesham), *Strange Land*, *Saint/Jeanne* and *Spring Awakening - The Musical* (Chelsea Theatre, London), *Cinderella, Carousel, Fame, Hairspray, Cabaret* and *Attempts On Her Life* (Amersham & Wycombe College), and Rouge28 Theatre's Japanese ghost story *Kwaidan* (UK tour), as well as Tayo Aluko's multi-award-winning monodrama *Call Mr Robeson* (touring the UK and internationally since 2007). Phil is proud to be an Associate Artist with director Gbemisola Ikumelo's Faith Drama Productions, for whom he has designed *The Fiddler* (Unicorn Theatre), *Next Door* (Cockpit Theatre), and short film *The Judge,* in addition to *Voices in the Alleyway* and *Yes, I Still Exist* (Spread Expression Dance) for movement director Cindy Claes.

Movement Director

Cindy Claes creates artistic earthquakes through her ground breaking dancehall, krumping and hip hop theatre productions. Choreographer, performer and dance storyteller, she tackles social and political issues through dance and theatre, creating rippling emotional reactions amongst her audiences, from laughter to tears. Challenging conversations are put centre stage with the potential to create positive social change through the arts. Credits include: *Prijs Roger Van de Voorde*, *Voices in the Alleyway*, *The Fiddler*, *Things aren't always Black or White*. Her unique international dance exchanges and leadership programmes, 1000 Pieces Puzzle, aim to raise awareness about social responsibility.

Lighting Designer

John Castle is a highly-skilled London-based lighting designer with experience in plays, musicals, touring and repertory productions, dance, education and pantomime. As well as lighting all sorts of projects John has lead the National Youth Theatre Technical Course, lectured at Amersham Collage, and runs his own company supplying technical support and innovation to the arts, JC Sound & Lighting Ltd. West End credits include: *Beginning To See The Light* for Jaybird Productions; *A Christmas Carol* for Talkwood Productions; *Chloe Can* for The National Youth Theatre; *You Can* for The National Youth Theatre.

Sound Designer/Production Manager

Michael Francis is an Australian freelance production and stage manager who has recently moved to London to enjoy the vibrant theatre industry here. A Bachelor Contemporary Music graduate, he has worked for many venues around Sydney as stage manager, production manager and sound designer, enjoying bringing productions to life through the technical and staging aspects. Previous production and technical work includes Sydney Theatre Company, Australian Theatre for Young People and Sydney Dance Company among others. He enjoys working on all manner of productions; however *Custody* has a particular appeal and effect due to the contemporary and poignant nature of the play.

Composer

Dan Bilbrough AKA Sekrit. The composer, drummer/ percussionist has been composing music since the age of 15 and has a number of production credits, most notably with hip hop acts such as Green Jade, Tor Cesay and Judah & Secret – under his previous alias DJ Secret Weapon – which have received national airplay and credible reviews. As well as working on his own solo projects Sekrit has recently been creating soundtracks for short films and theatre productions, including performing a live score at 2016s Shuffle Festival and also composing the recent trailer for 2017 BAFTA nominated film *Mouth Of Hell*.

Assistant Director

Eddie Howell has been working in theatre and film for the last 4 years, and has been involved in all areas of theatre and film from directing and writing to making smashing cups of tea for actors. He graduated from the BA Directing course at Drama Centre London in 2015 and has since worked as a producer and director with companies like Theatre N16, He started arts and theatre company Prevalent Grit in January 2016, which has been involved in supporting emerging talent from all artistic backgrounds. Eddie started working with FAITH Drama Productions on their 2016 season and was introduced to *Custody* then, and has continued to support the project until now.

Producer

Hannah Eugénie Tookey is a freelance theatre and film producer focussed on making work that tackles social and political issues. In 2016 she was awarded a Winston Churchill Memorial Trust Fellowship to travel to the USA and India to research how the arts can effectively combat and raise awareness about issues of social injustice. She is an alumnus of The Clore Emerging Leaders course, Stage One, and Raindance. Theatre credits include: *Dry Land* (Jermyn Street Theatre, Damsel Productions); *All The Little Lights* (UK Tour, Fifth Word); *Eggs* (Vault Festival, Orphee Productions) and *Astronauts of Hartlepool* (Vault Festival, Tim Foley). Film credits include: *Broken Meats* (Robin Linde Productions); and the London Calling funded short *Wargames* (working title). experience for the Australian, one which marks the start of his work in the United Kingdom.

Cast (in alphabetical order)

Kiké Brimah (SISTER) trained at ArtsEd and was most recently seen as Kayla in *The Riot Act* (Flatcap Films). Other TV/Film credits include *Love Type D* (Midnight Circus Films) and *Doctors* (BBC). Theatre credits include *Star in Some Other Mother* at The Traverse Theatre.

Sacharissa Claxton (LOVER) is an actor/writer/producer born and raised in Ipswich, Suffolk, now living in London. She trained at Identity School of Acting after receiving a 1st class BA (Hons) degree in Modern Drama Studies at Brunel University. Her credits include *Hound* (feature): *All of Me* (short); *Rive* (short); and *Out of Order* (musical). Sacharissa currently features in TV adverts for Johnson & Johnson and Vodafone.

Karlina Grace-Paşeda (MOTHER) Theatre credits include: *Death and the Kings Horseman* and *Welcome to* Thebes, both at The National Theatre; *SARAI*, a one-woman show at the Arcola Theatre; the title role in *Queen Poku* at the New Diorama Theatre; Shyanne in the two-hander *Trailer/trash*; the dual roles of Lincoln/Gloria in *Red Snapper* at the Belgrade Theatre, Coventry; Baptista in *Taming of the Shrew* at the Arts Theatre West End, Titania *in A Midsummer Night's Dream* at Blenheim Palace; and *The Asphalt Kiss*, also at The New Diorama Theatre. Other credits include *Macbeth*, *Bacchaefull* and *The Good Person of Setzuan*. Karlina trained at the Oxford School of Drama.

Urbain Hayo, also known as Urban Wolf, is artistic director of The Art Machine. He has primarily worked as an actor in the theatre, but has also ventured into writing, producing and performance art. His work focuses on telling stories that challenge and change society. *Custody* is Urbain's first produced play. He was moved to create it after watching the documentary film *Injustice*.

*

Urbain, Tom, Gbemisola and John would particularly like to thank the actors who performed in the R&D presentation of a studio version of *Custody* at Talawa in 2015: Faith Omole (SISTER), Chereen Buckley (LOVER), and Jacqueline Acheampong (MOTHER); and also, for embodying Brian in the rehearsals for this production, Dwane Walcott.

Thank you to: Ovalhouse, Arts Council England, Transform Newham, Unity Theatre Trust, Peggy Ramsay Foundation, Edge Fund; to Thomas Kell and Shabazz Graham; Joy Kisuka and Kaity Cornellier; Ken Fero; Marcia Rigg , Janet Alder and all the families from the Friends & Family Trust.

Custody was performed at Ovalhouse 28th March – 8th April 2017.

Tom Wainwright

CUSTODY

CAST

BROTHER   black male early 20s

SISTER   black female mid 20s

MOTHER   black female, early 50s

LOVER   female 20s

SON   black male 29*

CHORUS*

*To be performed by other members of the cast.

SETTING

Present day, over a two-year period.

ACT ONE

SCUFFLE

[can be repeated at any point where it would be effective]

CHORUS   There.

There was.

There was a.

There was a bit.

There was a bit of.

There was a bit of a scuffle.

And.

There was a bit of a scuffle and, I'm sorry.

I'm sorry.

I'm sorry to say.

There was a bit of a scuffle and I'm sorry to say.

He .

He passed.

Away.

He passed away.

He passed away.

He passed away.

He passed away.

EULOGY

BROTHER   Me and you Brian, we do everything together.
Football , comics, video games, whatever.
I'm the clown, getting into fights
shooting off my mouth
But you.
You're smooth.

SISTER   I come round on a Friday night and there you
       are,

glass of white wine and
'This is my tune,' you say, and turn it up loud,
smiling as the window-frames rattle.
You're a good looking man.

BROTHER   Taking longer to get ready than your girl...

ALL   Amen!

LOVER   I watch you from our bed as you run your
        electric razor for
the seventeenth time across your jaw.
Skin stretched, flawless.
I tease you: 'You'll get shaving bumps.'
You say, 'Ey, all this didn't just happen by acci-
    dent, you know.'
I throw something soft at you.
You turn.
Come towards...
Pin me down...
I let you...

MOTHER   My favourite.

BROTHER/SISTER   Oi!

MOTHER   *Well...*
My first born
and you slept!
Times there were I'd wait for you to wake
your own self up.
Peeping round the door,
Love drunk on your snoring.

Ribs rising and falling.
Your open prone perfect throat.
You were an early walker, a bit of a late talker.
Unlike these two who jabbered from the get-
    go.

BROTHER/SISTER Mum!

MOTHER   [To SISTER] Especially you.
               I'd barely batted my eyes before
               you'd turned into a girl-woman
               with your own ideas and your own wardrobe...

SISTER   'You're not going out like that young lady!'

BROTHER   And boom!
               It's on.

SISTER   What? What's wrong with this?

MOTHER   I can see right up your thigh, for goodness sake.

SISTER   So?

MOTHER   Don't you 'so' me,
               Put another top on – *I can see everything!*

SISTER   I can wear what I want.

MOTHER   And every man can *see* the hell what he want.

SISTER   I'm fifteen years old, I can take care of myself.

Custody

MOTHER   [Laughs]

SISTER   What you laughing for?

MOTHER   Because you don't know anything about anything! You're a child.

SISTER   [Kisses her teeth]

MOTHER   [Ballistic, grabbing SISTER] Don't you dare do that in my face – Girl, I
brought you into this world and I will take you out of it!

BROTHER   Step up Brian like a Jedi Knight.
'A problem here there is not.'

SISTER   I feel this arm drape over my shoulder. It's you.
'Sister – you look beautiful. All grown up, a real woman.
I know you can handle yourself
But she doesn't.
And she'll be up all night worrying herself sick
because the world is full of dangers, and she loves you
more than you can ever know,
so sister, please, for love, go and change that outfit.'

BROTHER   *'The Force is Strong In You'*

SISTER   And I find myself floating up the stairs to my room.

Taking off my Nicki Minaj.
Putting on jeans and a cardigan.
How do you always find a way to make peace
    break out?
It's your gift. To the world.
My gorgeous, gentle big brother.

BROTHER   My brother.

MOTHER   My son.

LOVER   My lover.

BROTHER   Me and you Brian, we did everything to
            gether...

ALL   [Soft] Amen.

THE KNOCK

[SISTER, BROTHER and LOVER are laughing]

LOVER   I'm like, 'shave it off' –

        He's like,
        'You don't understand, I'll be thirty in a week.'
         I'm like 'it's sexy!'
        He's like
        'How is going bald sexy?'
        I'm like,
        'Larry Fishburne, Samuel L Jackson, Isaac
            Hayes...'
        he's like

'these are *old men*'
 I'm like
'Tupac – he's cute'
he's like
'*Tupac?!* He's dead.'

[HUGE BANG AT THE DOOR. LOVER gets up]

[LOVER answers the door]

LOVER   Hello?

            [To us] High Vis.
            Sweet sweat.
            Grey eyes.
            Thick neck.
            Aftershave.
            Black hair.
            Boots. Stubble. Crackle.
            Fat fingers.
            Hairs on the knuckles.
            Polyester.
            Keeps his hat on.
            Cheap watch.
            Wedding ring.
            Licks lips.
            Lips move.

MOTHER GETS NEWS

[SISTER, BROTHER and LOVER at MOTHER's house]

MOTHER   What has happened?

7

SISTER   Mum. Brian's died.

MOTHER   What?

SISTER   The police –

MOTHER   Why are you talking about the police?

SISTER   They stopped him/and

MOTHER   What are you saying?

SISTER   I'm saying he's died.
            Mum. Brian's died.

MOTHER   Something is burning. On the stove.

[MOTHER goes through to kitchen, slams door. SISTER goes to follow. BROTHER stops her]

MOTHER   [To us] I have guests tonight.

            I have Sandra. And Lewis. And Janet from
              church.

            I am making rice and talapia.

            I am halfway through descaling the fish.

            Thyme

            Two Maggi cubes

            All purpose

            Onion

Pepper

Plum tomato

Two cups of water.

Stir.
Lid.

Simmer.

[Pause]

What just happened, Brian?

INTERROGATION

[The next day]

SISTER   'Independent Police Complaints Commission,'
            she's saying.

MOTHER   ...you are stopped at eleven thirty...

BROTHER   ...a routine stop and search...

SISTER   ...behave aggressively...

MOTHER   ...officers are called...

LOVER   [To us] Now you're in the van.
            Now you're falling down.
            But your heart – your sweet heart – is still beat-
                ing.

MOTHER   [To us] At three forty five this morning you are
           pronounced dead.

[Silence]

SISTER   [To IPCC] Why is my brother not alive right
                now?

LOVER   When can I see him?

SISTER   Was he suffocated?
           You said he was restrained.
           How was he restrained?

BROTHER   Why was he restrained?

LOVER   Who restrained him?

SISTER   Did you separate the officers?

BROTHER   Why not?

SISTER   Did you seal off the area?

BROTHER   *The area where my brother died.*

SISTER   What time?

BROTHER   Answer the question.

LOVER   *What were you doing for four hours?*

CHORUS   '...we had to work on the press release.'

PRESS RELEASE

CHORUS   'At 11:30 pm two officers from the Metropoli-
              tan Police
          Flagged down
          A large 29 year old IC3 male
          In a silver BMW they had reason to suspect was
              stolen,
          In Deptford, South London,
          To carry out a routine stop and search.
          The male, who is believed to be linked with a
              number of criminal gangs,
          Resisted arrest,
          Behaving violently and aggressively,
          And was possibly intoxicated.
          Back-up was called,
          And three more officers arrived on the scene;
          The suspect was handcuffed and taken to Brix-
              ton Police Station.
          The male was escorted through to the custody
              suite where it
          collapsed and appeared to lose consciousness.
          Officers at the scene attempted to resuscitate
              the male;
          An ambulance was called to take it to King's
              College Hospital,
          Where it later died without regaining con-
              sciousness.
          The exact sequence of events is to be the sub-
              ject
          Of an IPCC investigation.'

ID

[Two days later. LOVER, BROTHER AND SISTER are viewing/
identifying the body]

SISTER   [To us] It's cold in here.

              Mum won't come.
              She's ashamed.

              [Looks down at table]

              It's you.
              It's not you.

              I should cry.
              I can't.
              I won't
              Not here.
              Not now.
              I want blood.
              I want justice.
              I want a cigarette.

              I'm signing the consent forms –
              There's a copper.
              Standing. Staring.
              What's she doing here?

              [To COPPER] Why are you here?
              [To us] Nothing.
              Just standing. Staring.

[To MORTUARY TECHNICIAN] Can I see him
    from the other side?
Can you unzip the bag?
I wanna see my brother's body – not one side
    of his face

BROTHER   Why's he up against the wall?

SISTER   [To us] 'To preserve his dignity,' this copper-
               pot's saying.

BROTHER   Just unzip the bag!

SISTER   [To us] They're saying they can't do that.

BROTHER   [To us] The mortuary technician's acting all
               shook.

SISTER   I want to see my brother's body now.
           No, don't look at her, man, I'm asking
           You.

BROTHER   She's not shouting – you're the one who's
               shouting
           How am I not calm?
           You wanna see not calm?
           No that's not a threat.
           What you talkin on your fuckin radio for?

SISTER   Mind his language?
           He's just lost his brother – and you want him to
               mind his language?
           [She moves along wall to look]

13

What am I doing?
I'm getting a better view.
Yes I can
And I am
Get out my face.
What's that?
WHAT IS THAT?
THAT HUGE MASSIVE SWELLING ON HIS HEAD

BROTHER   WHAT IS THAT?

SISTER   WHAT DID YOU DO TO HIM?

BROTHER   I SWEAR TO GOD MAN, SOMEONE'S GONNA
PAY FOR THIS!

SISTER   GET YOUR FILTHY HANDS OFF ME!

BROTHER   DON'T TOUCH HER!

SISTER   YOU KILLED HIM!
YOU KILLED HIM!
YOU KILLED MY BROTHER!

CHURCH

[In church, the first Sunday after Brian's death. Prayers, Songs.]

MOTHER   Nothing.
There is nothing here.
I have never really needed Him before and now
that I do

He is absent.
I am full of absence.
My womb aches with nothingness –
Where is He?
Is He afraid, ashamed? Is He embarrassed?
What a time to run away with His tail between
     His legs.
Where is He?
Is this what He does?
Remove mothers' sons and then run?

[MOTHER leaves, followed by BROTHER, SISTER and LOVER]

LOVER AT HOME ALONE

LOVER   [To us] I'm not staying.
               I can't stay here.
               Just came to get some underwear.
               Then back to your mum's.

               You've got mail...

               [She opens letter]

               'Hello Brian,

               *It's good to know that with Barclaycard,
               whether you spend online or on the high street,
               your payments are protected as standard.*

               Here's a reminder of how you're protected:

               *Peace of mind comes as standard when you pay
               with Barclaycard. Should your purchases be*

*faulty, damaged or don't arrive at all, you could
be covered. It's a little secret weapon all credit
cards come with.*

*We're always working behind the scenes to
protect you from fraud. But if it does happen,
your money will be refunded, including any in-
terest you've paid. Simply let us know and we'll
get it sorted, pronto.'*

[She breaks down]

ADMIN

MOTHER   I cannot bury my son?

SISTER   [To us] Somehow Mum's making this my fault.
            [To MOTHER] How much money have you got?

MOTHER   You want money.
            Always you want money.

SISTER   [To BROTHER] I guess you're broke?

BROTHER   I'm not *broke*.
            What it is, yeah, is I'm waitin...

SISTER   [To us] I tell her how much and she's saying,

MOTHER   *WHAT?!*

SISTER   ...plus solicitor fees, post-mortem,
              and then there's the funeral...

MOTHER   No funeral.

BROTHER   No funeral?

MOTHER   No body no funeral.

SISTER   We won't get him til after the Inquest,
              Mum –
              That could be, I don't know...
              Months.

MOTHER   Why?

SISTER   I thought I'd explained...
              [To us] I thought I'd explained.

MOTHER   Explain again.
              Explain to me how they can kill my son and
                    then prevent me from burying him.
              I am listening.

SISTER   [To us] I am explaining.

              I think she finally gets it.

MOTHER   I still do not understand.

SISTER   Are you on your phone?

BROTHER   [He is] No.

17

SISTER   Jesus.

BROTHER   I wasn't!

SISTER   [To MOTHER] But we could do something.
             In the meantime.
             A memorial.

MOTHER   No.

SISTER   I don't understand.

MOTHER   This is shameful.
             I am having nothing to do with this.
             I am busy.

BROTHER   *Busy?* Busy doing what?

MOTHER   Don't you give me backchat.

BROTHER   I just...

MOTHER   *You* need to sort this out. *You*.

[She starts leaving]

BROTHER   Where are you going?

MOTHER   I am going to buy some shoes.
             Then I am going to get my hair done.
             And then I think I will go to the cinema.
             We're out of milk.
             Rectify this.

[She goes. SISTER and BROTHER alone. She shoves him. He shoves her back.]

MEMORIAL

[Two weeks later. MOTHER's house]

SISTER   [To LOVER] Take these through.

[LOVER takes food out]

CHORUS   Mmm, delicious. And the food looks good too.

[Huge belly laugh at his own joke]

LOVER   [To us] Three weeks, Brian.
           You still haven't put your keys in the door
           Hit the blue top full fat straight from the bottle
           Man I hate how you do that.
           How you did that.
           Brian, baby, I loved how you did that.
           [To CHORUS] Get off!
           [To us] I'm getting perved on by a massive Afri-
               can –
           wearing a... tent.
           I think he's your uncle –
           Everyone's your uncle
           So it seems
           And your sister's got me handing out snacks

[CHORUS slaps her arse, she grabs his hand]

LOVER   Do that again and I'll kill you.

CHORUS   Whoa, this one has got fire in her belly, hehe!

SISTER   I need some help in the kitchen.

CHORUS   [A different one] May I have this dance?

LOVER   No you may not.

CHORUS   You would deny a grieving uncle?

LOVER   Yes I would.

SISTER   I need help over here.

LOVER   Yes, in a minute.

SISTER   I need you now.

LOVER   [To us] If this was a year later,
          We'd be married,
          I'd be your wife.
          I'd be the one bossing *her* around.

SISTER   Mind yourself –

LOVER   [To us] Instead I'm ghosting round your fake
              funeral.
          No body, no mother
          Your mum's gone away
          for the weekend.
          I don't get it.
          Everyone's talking about Olayinka.
          Who's Olayinka?

20

Where's Brian?
Where are you?
And when you coming back – this isn't funny
    anymore.

CHORUS   Young lady, what time do you get off?

LOVER   What?

CHORUS   What time do you finish?

LOVER   I'm not a *waitress* - I'm family.

CHORUS   You knew Olayinka?

LOVER   I'm Brian's fiancée.
    [To us]
    I could grab this tray and smash it over his fat
        head.
    Scream
    'This isn't Brian!
    It's not him.
    I am him. I am. Not you.
    He collects hi-top sneakers, he supports Crystal
    Palace,
    He's an absolute diva when he's hungry.'
    Aren't you?
    Do *they* know this?
    Do *they* know you?
    No, I do, and I'm handing out drinks.

*

LOVER'S FLAT

[Later, with BROTHER. LOVER's on a sofa.]

BROTHER   You alright?

LOVER   Get me a drink.

BROTHER   What?

LOVER   Something strong.

[He comes back with two drinks. Pause]

BROTHER   Are you gonna be alright here?

LOVER   No.

BROTHER   Is it not a bit weird?

LOVER   What?

BROTHER   Here.

LOVER   Yeah.

[Silence]

BROTHER   D'you want me to go?

LOVER   Yeah.

[BROTHER goes to leave]

LOVER   Hold me.

BROTHER   ...

LOVER   Hold me.

[BROTHER awkwardly does so. She laughs]

BROTHER   What you laughin for?

LOVER   You know how to hold a woman don't you?

BROTHER   Yeah.

LOVER   Well then hold me.
[He hugs her from behind]
Tighter.
Tell me about him.

BROTHER   Like what?

LOVER   Anything.
When you were kids.

BROTHER   Well, there was this one time...

LOVER   [To us] He is telling me the most...
Revolting story of how you
Took him to the funfair when you were twelve,
And he was... sick everywhere.
Why is he telling me this?
Your brother...

BROTHER   *'...your Mum's a crackhead...'*

LOVER   ...You're here again... just for a moment
He smells like you
Feels like you.

BROTHER   ...fucking cover them boys head to foot in
nasty five year old toffee apple candy floss hot
doggy vomit. Boom. In your face. The carny
curses us out and then we leg it. Funny as hell,
man.

LOVER   That.
Is disgusting.

[Silence]

LOVER   You can go now.

[BROTHER starts to wriggle out. LOVER turns around and
kisses him. BROTHER pulls away.]

BROTHER   What? Nah.

[LOVER kisses him again. He kisses her back. They have sex.
She comes. Is disgusted. Pushes him away]

LOVER   Go.

BROTHER   ...

LOVER   GO!

MOTHER/SON 1

SON   Mum.

MOTHER   Son?

SON   Hi Mum.

MOTHER   My son. Are you OK?

SON   I can't sleep.

MOTHER   Have you tried reading a book?

SON   Doesn't work.

MOTHER   Have you tried counting sheep?

SON   Doesn't work.

MOTHER   Have you tried breathing in through your nose and out through your mouth?

SON   Doesn't work.

MOTHER   Have you tried not trying?

SON   Doesn't work.

MOTHER   When you close your eyes, do you see patterns?

SON   Yes.

MOTHER   Good.
              Watch these patterns and soon they will turn
                   into pictures.
              Yes?
              Are you doing this?

SON   Yes.

MOTHER   What do you see?

SON   Nothing.
              Here there is nothing.
              Just me.

MOTHER   How you say?

SON   There's no way through.
              I can't pass.

MOTHER   I don't understand...

SON   I can't move.

MOTHER   Are you afraid?

SON   Yes.

MOTHER   What will you do?

SON   I will hope.

MOTHER   My baby...

SON   Mum, will you sing to me?

[She sings to him]

ACT TWO

INQUEST

[Three months later. They are all waiting to leave MOTHER's house]

SISTER   Are you serious?

BROTHER   What?

SISTER   You're going like that?

BROTHER   What's wrong with this?

SISTER   Look at you!

BROTHER   [To us] She's giving me bare grief.
              Thinks I should be wearing a suit.

SISTER   You've had three months to get your shit
                 together
              And –

BROTHER   [To SISTER] I thought you could wear what you
                 want.

SISTER   I can. Mum can. She can.
              Not you.

BROTHER   Why not?

SISTER   You're Brian.
            To the jury.
            They see you, they see him.

LOVER   I think you look fine.

SISTER   He does not look fine.

MOTHER   Could you not even manage shoes?

SISTER   They're gonna look at you
            And think
            'Criminal.'

BROTHER   I'll get changed.

SISTER   There's no time.
            Get in the car.

[They get in the car. SISTER drives]

SISTER   Now remember, everyone, this isn't a criminal
                court.
            No one's on trial.
            This is just to establish
            Who Brian was.
            Where he died.
            When he died
            How he died...

BROTHER   [To us] She's enjoying this.

Look at her.

SISTER   [To BROTHER] And you take that look off your
            face.

BROTHER   Oh my days
            Now you got a problem with my face?

SISTER   Always.

MOTHER   Leave your brother alone.

SISTER   You got the photo, Mum?

[MOTHER clutches it]

[They arrive at the Coroner's Court]

BROTHER   That's it?
            That's it?
            We've been waiting three months for this?
            Looks like a pub.

INQUEST – THE NEXT DAY

LOVER   I never knew how fragile you were
            When you sauntered out the house last au-
                tumn
            Humming some cheesy rnb track,
            Out of tune
            Out of date – you know you really can't sing –
                never could

29

I didn't realise you weren't coming back,
I didn't realise just minutes from your own
        front door
That you would get stopped in your
Own car
And strangled –
Sorry, my mistake
Suffer from postural asphyxia
Sorry, my mistake.
What really happened was that your heart
        stopped beating.
Just like that.
One minute it's beating.
The next it's not.
And you just drop
Down dead.
Sudden Cardiac Death.
Even bullshit has a fancy name somewhere.
Sorry, my mistake.
I don't know how you died.

Everyone else seems to.
They're all so alive.

INQUEST – TWO WEEKS LATER

BROTHER   [To us] Two weeks we've been here.
           Man, I'm bored!
           I can't bring my phone in so I have to like...
               listen.
           I've fallen asleep a couple of times.
           Snored.

SISTER   She's nice – the coroner – youngish.
          Looks at you like you're a human.
          She's saying something...

CHORUS   '...could be distressing for family members...'

LOVER   [To us] Something about

CHORUS   '...CCTV...'

LOVER   [To us] I don't know if I can watch this....

CHORUS   '...then leave now...'

LOVER   [To us] You are being marched semi-conscious
          into the police station.

BROTHER   [To us] You are being moved into a cell.

SISTER   [To us] You are falling to the ground.

MOTHER   [To us] You are hauling yourself up.

LOVER   [To us] Your trousers are falling down.

BROTHER   [To us] Officers are laughing at you.

LOVER   [To us] They are pointing at your arse.
          One officer is gyrating his hips

SISTER   [To us] You are falling to the ground.

MOTHER   [To us] You are not getting back up.

LOVER   [To us] Officers are ignoring you.

BROTHER   Stop ignoring him!

LOVER   [To us] Paying attention now.

SISTER   [To us] Officers are panicking.

LOVER   [To us] Officers are calling an ambulance.

SISTER   [To us] Officers are trying to resuscitate you.

BROTHER   [To us] Pumping your chest.

LOVER   [To us] Breathing in your mouth.

SISTER   [To us] They're covered in sweat.

LOVER   [To us] Officers are looking around.
          Officers are trying again.
          And again.
          And again.
          And again.

[MOTHER runs out. BROTHER follows]

[Outside. BROTHER bearhugs MOTHER. She starts hitting
him. He tries to restrain her – she pulls away]

MOTHER   It should be you in there.
          If I could swap him for you I would do it
          Like that.

[MOTHER goes back inside]

MOTHER/SON 2

SON   Hi Mum.

MOTHER   My son!

SON   Hi.

MOTHER   You still cannot sleep?

SON   I've got a man on me.
            Three men.

MOTHER   What are they doing?

SON   Cuffing my hands behind my back.

MOTHER   What else are they doing?

SON   Pushing my face into the ground.

MOTHER   What else are they doing?

SON   Crushing my neck.

MOTHER   What else are they doing?

SON   Breaking my ribs.

MOTHER   What else are they doing?

SON   Screaming
They're terrified.
They smell of McDonalds.

MOTHER   What are they screaming?

SON   They're screaming at me not to move.

MOTHER   Are you moving?

SON   I can't move.

MOTHER   Have you told them?

SON   I can't breathe.
Can't speak to tell them that
I can't breathe.
Eyes rolling in my skull
Like a fruit machine
Lighting up
Tripping out
Paying out
Change Clattering
Cherry Cherry, Cherry
Bar, Bar, Bar
Seven, Seven, Seven
Nudge...

MOTHER   Do you want me to sing to you?

SON   I want to be with my father.
And his father.
And his father.

Instead I'm stuck here with these terrified men
Who stink of milk and Big Macs.
I wish they'd get off me.

MOTHER   What can I do?

SON   Get these men off me.
          Get these men off me
          I can't breathe...

BROTHER LETS RIP

BROTHER   [To us] You always were her favourite, weren't
              ya?
          Brian or his good for nothing brother?
          Hands down bruv, fair enough
          I can't begrudge you the love that she poured
          heart and soul into your blood –
          The same love
          That was skipped on the loud mental kid
          Who got so excited
          When the X-Men theme tune started he wasn't
          allowed to watch it.
          Whose main motto in life is
          'Ah fuck it.'
          Who once got a C
          For art –
          His best mark in a school career marked by
              failure.
          'Mum, Mum – look I got a C.'
          'Hush your mouth boy, your brother got an A
              star.'

Course he did.
No flies on that bookworm prick.
No slang for
Clean as a whistle no booze no fags my body is
    a temple
Brian.
Apple of his mother's eye
Apple of the *world's* eye
Everybody give it up for Brian!
What is it that you got that I don't?
Other than...
Brains, Looks, Class, Style, Self-respect, Money,
    Status, a Fiancée, Property, Your Own Busi-
    ness
that BMW.
Fair play, bruv. I'm proud of you. I look up to
you. What else can I do?
But I tell you one thing I've got on you...
I'm blacker than you.
Oh yeah.
I sound blacker, I look blacker, I walk blacker, I
    dress blacker –
hell I probably *fuck* blacker than you –
ask your girl.
'But the clients don't like it they get frightened
    by that black shit.'
Hey – go for it.
Do what you gotta do –
Man's gotta get that paper somehow, innit
    bruv?
And if what it takes is selling out your own self
    so you can get that cheddar
you *wear* them skinny jeans – I got my belt un-
    der my arse

You *shop* at Waitrose – I'm down Iceland
You *go* them arthouse cinemas and stroke your
beard wanking over some
foreign film about pigeons in fuckin... Albania –
I'll be watching Iron Man 5 – in 3D – with a
popcorn the size of a dustbin
Fuckin coconut.
Yeah, you heard me – sell-out bitch.
Where'd that bounty shit even get you any-
    way?
Strangled in a van by some white boys
probably beggin for your life like a fuckin
Pussy.
I'm glad you're gone.
Monkey off my motherfuckin back.

INQUEST – THE NEXT DAY

SISTER   This is it, bro
            They've made their decision.
            Unlawful Killing and we're laughing.
            Not Death by Misadventure
            Not Narrative Verdict
            Not Open Verdict
            Not Gross Negligence
            Un-law-ful Killing.
            That's what we need to put these bastards in-
                side.
            The foreman's standing, shuffling his papers
            Come on, just say it
            Say the words: 'Unlawful Killing'
            Do it just do it just *fucking* do it.

LOVER   Lips move.

[Pause. Register. They celebrate and go crazy. LOVER breaks off while the others continue]

LOVER   Look at them
              Jumping up and down like you've come back to
                life
              Brian jumping out the grave like a rocking ga-
                zelle
              But you're not
              Are you?
              You're just as gone as you were before.
              But now we have to fight
              For months. Years.
              I don't want to fight, baby
              I want to grieve.
              B, baby, I want you to leave.

FUNERAL

[Two weeks later]

BROTHER   Yo, bro, don't take this the wrong way, but
              you're takin your time
              To die.
              Four months bro
              And now we bury you.
              Lazy.
              Just sayin...

MOTHER   Why don't you come to me anymore?

Please come.
Tell me how you are.
I will stay up with you.
We can talk.
Are those men still on you?

SISTER   I've seen their faces.
I know where they are.
I'm taking those bastards down, Brian.

LOVER   Want you B.
Want you inside me.
Feel your weight
Your back
You.

BROTHER   Yeah, look, about what happened with your
        girl...
I'm sorry, man.
That shit was fucked up.

[He starts giggling]

SISTER   What's the matter with you?

BROTHER   *I can't help it.*

SISTER   Why are you laughing?

BROTHER   *I don't know.*

MOTHER   Stop it. Stop this at once.

BROTHER   *I'm trying.*

LOVER   What's *funny?*

BROTHER   *Oh God!*

LOVER   I'm funny am I? This is funny?

BROTHER   *No. Stop talking.*

SISTER   Shame on you. Shame.

BROTHER   *I can't stop it, it won't stop.*

MOTHER   *Make* it stop.

BROTHER   *I can't.*

MOTHER   You are a disgrace.

BROTHER   *This is horrible.*

[They all start laughing]

INSUFFICIENT EVIDENCE

[The next day. SISTER with letter in hand]

SISTER   'Insufficient evidence to prosecute.'
           And that's that. All those months of work un-
                  done.

MOTHER   Insufficient...
              But there is a video —

SISTER   I know...

MOTHER   They are laughing while they watch him die.

SISTER   I know.

MOTHER   There are eyewitness statements who say that
              these men
              kicked him and kicked him and kicked him and
              kicked him —

SISTER   Mum. I know.

MOTHER   And *this* is insufficient?

SISTER   It would seem so.

MOTHER   *It would seem so?*

BROTHER   So what do we do now?

SISTER   We fight little brother.
              Have you got that in you?
              We fight til we drop and I don't feel like
                 dropping
              cos a letter says we better go quietly.
              [To us] Brian, I'm not going anywhere.
              I'm staying right here
              I'm making shitloads of noise
              I'm banging doors

Cracking skulls
Upsetting applecarts
An upstart getting
Mad awkward.
Got a pain in the arse?
That'll be me.
Getting right up your nose?
That'll be me.
Thorn in your side?
Yep, that'll be me.
And if you're going out your mind
Well then, that'll be me.
I'm not just bringin it
I'm takin and sellin it
and makin me
A big fat profit on
Rage.
I'm goin all out now
I will have justice
I will have vengeance
Have their heads on
Sticks
Started?
Allow that, Brian.
I'm not even warmed up yet.

MOTHER/SON 3

[That evening]

SON   Mum.

Custody

MOTHER   Brian?

SON   Hi Mum.

MOTHER   You came back!

SON   ...

MOTHER   How are you?

SON   ...

MOTHER   You have made it?

SON   ...

MOTHER   I knew you would.

SON   ...

MOTHER   How is your father?

SON   ...

MOTHER   Don't tell me – he is in his allotment – boasting about the size of his marrow. Hm?

SON   ...

MOTHER   I have seen bigger.

SON   ...

MOTHER   Brian? Are you OK?

SON   Cherry cherry cherry
          Seven Seven
          Bar Bar
          Milk
          Bananas, Bananas, Bananas, Bananas
          Watermelon, Horseshoe, Diamond, Pear
          Big Win, Big Win
          Orange, Four Leafed Clover
          Kiwi, Orange, Orange, Lemon,
          Bunch of Blueberries
          Mcflurry, Mcflurry
          Milk, Lucozade, Lynx
          Sweat Roll
          Hold down
          Nudge
          Watermelon
          Seven
          Can't breathe, Can't see
          Can't move, can't scream
          Big Win Big Mac
          Coins stacked
          Neck snapped
          Strength sapped
          Face slapped
          Eyes black with blood
          Veins burst
          Fruit burst
          Last spurt of living
          Giving way, giving way, going going going gone
          And I'm gone
          I'm gone.
          I'm gone.

MOTHER   Brian?

SON   Cherry cherry cherry Seven Seven Bar Bar
            Milk
        Bananas Bananas, Bananas, Bananas
        Watermelon, Horseshoe, Diamond, Pear
        Big Win, Big Win –

[MOTHER screams]

ACT THREE

MOTHER PRAYS FOR BRIAN'S SAFE PASSAGE

[MOTHER performs ritual, and makes offering to deity of
sweets, marbles etc]

MOTHER   To the Lord of All Paths, opener of doors,
            pathfinder, illustrious warrior,
        I offer this humble prayer...
        I ask Olofin God to bless you, Elegbara,
        He who begins and ends all things
        And all things between the dead and the living
        I ask Olofin God to bless you, Elegbara.
        Ashe.
        Elegbara, my son is imprisoned.
        He is not free to be at peace in harmony
        With the Ancestors.
        He cannot pass.
        He is restricted
        Constricted
        Unable to move on to the land of the dead

Unable to return to the living
Haunting me.
He is in agony.
Please, Elegbara,
With humble respect,
I ask
That you clear a path
For my son
So that he may pass.

SISTER CAMPAIGNING

[Weeks later. Mic in hand, SISTER is addressing a campaigning event in barnstorming style]

SISTER   Let me break it down for you.

                Your son, brother, father, whatever
                Dies in police custody.
                The IPCC officer investigating your case
                Fails to separate the arresting officers
                Key evidence is lost
                Through incompetence or outright
                        obstruction...

BROTHER   [To us] Our little sister, raisin hell
                Lovin this
                attention and applause
                Fuckin diva.
                None of this has got shit to do with you.
                Black man at risk from the white
                Po-lice?

Custody

What's new?
Not this.
This is bullshit.
Shoulda kept your head down, bro
Kept a low profile
But nah, you couldn't do that – too much ego.
You were askin for it.

SISTER   A press release goes out hours later
claiming your son, brother, father, whatever
was a drug dealer,
a gangster,
behaving aggressively,
And that he was powerfully built and big.
Always, always big.
The police follow, intimidate you
You feel like *you're* the one on trial
And you are.
At the inquest invariably the coroner will be
A white middle-aged male,
He instructs the jury to find a verdict of
Death by Misadventure.
In common parlance:
Shit happens.
But let's say you get lucky and you actually get
a verdict of
Unlawful Killing.
You go crazy, get drunk on
Revenge and justice
But this is
A False Dawn.
For no sooner are you mounting a compelling
case
Than a letter arrives and bluntly explains

There is insufficient evidence to prosecute
Due in no small part
To the farcical investigation in the immediate
aftermath
Of your loved one's death
Carried out by the IPCC officer –
Remember her?
Who by coincidence turns out to be an ex-
copper
And white.
This happens and will happen
Every time
And we need to change this *now*!

BROTHER   [To us] Change what?
Ain't nothing gonna change.
Don't even know what I'm doing here.

BROTHER IN CLUB

BROTHER   [To us] See this, bruv, this is my scene
Bare shoulders, bare pussy, bare glow in the
    dark teeth.
[To a punter]
Yes, bro, you want some Mandy?
Yeah, I got coke
You wanna talk to your mates?
Sure, do your thing, bro.
[To us] See, I'm friendly Brian.
Look at me, being friendly.
You laughing, bro?
Sneering down your nose?

Custody

Here's my man, back again,
He looks shook,
Like I'm gonna hurt him.
Cos I do that Brian
When I'm not here shottin in clubs
I'm a thug
Collecting debts
For a badman with a alias.
Knocking down doors and breaking bones
It takes bottle.
Not anyone can do it.
You couldn't, man.
You'd get hurt.
So you can sit there and smirk
On your fluffy white cloud
But man I'm down here on earth
Trying to live.
Trying to maintain.
It ain't easy.
So go easy
On me.
[to punter] Boom - there you go.
[to us] Just a posh kid buying Charlie.
It's all good.
And then he does that
They all do that
Puts on a weird voice and tries to talk black.
'Safe, man.'
Safe?
And the mad thing is I think it's for
My benefit.
This boy feels the need to be more like this?
This
Streak of drug dealing piss?

Thought that'd make you laugh, bro.
That there's for you.
And while you're sniggering
I'll be living.

MOTHER PUTS HEAT ON SISTER

MOTHER   What is the delay?
Why always am I waiting for you
to tell me
what is coming next?

SISTER   Cos I'm the only one who's on top of all this.

MOTHER   Don't patronise me –

SISTER   I'm not.

MOTHER   You are and I don't like it.
I want my day in the High Court

SISTER   Sure –

MOTHER   Do not 'sure' me young lady –

SISTER   *I'm trying to explain –*

MOTHER   Try harder.

SISTER   The appeals process takes time...

MOTHER   We do not have time.

Custody

Brian does not have time.

SISTER   Er... what?

MOTHER   You heard me.

SISTER   I heard
the words.
Doesn't mean I understood.

MOTHER   He comes to me
At night.

SISTER   You've been dreaming – so have I –

MOTHER   This is not dreaming
He is pleading with me
Screaming oftentimes
To prise these men off his back
He cannot breathe...

SISTER   OK.

MOTHER   Not OK.
He needs me to find him a pathway.

SISTER   To where?

MOTHER   To the ancestors!

SISTER   OK.

MOTHER   Not OK!

SISTER   Mum, wherever Brian's gone he's in a good
                  place.

MOTHER   You have no authority to say as such.
                 You know nothing of this.
                 He is imprisoned, confined, constricted –

SISTER   I know the video was horrific –

MOTHER   I am not talking of a video
                 I am talking of my son –
                 Your brother
                 His spirit is
                 Frozen
                 Going nowhere.
                 We need to release him.
                 You need to release him.
                 Bring those men to trial.
                 Only then will he find his way home.
                 [pause]
                 I should never have brought us here
                 Into the dragon's lair.

SISTER   Steady on –

MOTHER   We are hated.
                 By their people.
                 By their God.

SISTER   [Looking around] Are you still going to church?
                 What is this stuff?

MOTHER   Offerings.

To *our* Gods. To the Orishas.
Elegbara. Yemoja.
I should never have turned my back on what
    we are.
Brian would still be here.
This is my fault.

SISTER   It's not.

MOTHER   I need to pray for your brother.
              Join me.

SISTER   I don't know Mum – it's not really my thing.

MOTHER   And what is?
              What do you have beyond the facts that you
                  know?
              You are lost, little girl.
              Now go.
              But remember.
              You made a promise.
              That you would deliver justice.
              And I intend to keep you to it.

SISTER   You can't put that on me.

MOTHER   I have and I will.
              Do not fail your brother.
              Do not.
              Do not.

*

WHERE'VE YOU BEEN?

SISTER   Where've you been?
I never see you at Mum's.
You do still live there, right?

BROTHER   Right.

SISTER   Right.
Don't you think she needs a little looking after?

BROTHER   By me?

SISTER   By anyone.
She's just been bangin on about Orisha and offerings
and Brian being lost and visiting her and...

BROTHER   And what?

SISTER   Does that not alarm you?
That our God-fearing mum's
Ripped up her bible and leaving palm oil
And cigars for Elegbara?

BROTHER   It's all bollocks anyway.

SISTER   *Er, you think?*
The point is, Little Brother, she thinks it's real.

BROTHER   What d'you want me to do about it?

SISTER   *Maybe talk to her?!*

BROTHER   I'm not normally here.

SISTER   Where are you?

BROTHER   When?

SISTER   When you're not here?!

BROTHER   Around.

SISTER   Around? Where?

BROTHER   Literally where?

SISTER   Yeah.

BROTHER   Er, alright.
          The studio.

SISTER   What studio?

BROTHER   *Er*, a studio where you make music.

SISTER   You can't sing you can't dance
          What are you doing in a studio?

BROTHER   I'm a MC.

SISTER   [laughing] You?
          Really?

BROTHER   Yeah.

SISTER   Come on then, show me.
            Spit some bars, fam.

BROTHER   What, now?

SISTER   Yes, now.

BROTHER   [leaving] Fuck this.

SISTER   Pussy.

BROTHER   What the fuck?

SISTER   What you gonna do?

BROTHER   ...

SISTER   Nothing.
            What you doing for money?

BROTHER   I told you.

SISTER   How are you earning money?

BROTHER   Event nights. Music.

SISTER   Who you tryin to fool boy
            You don't do music
            You don't have it in you
            You're just small time
            Small fry,
            Yeah you're that guy who hangs round in clubs
            Aren't you?

BROTHER   ...

SISTER   Well, that's about all you're good for.
Our brother was the one thing keeping you
    straight –

BROTHER   What has this got to do with Brian?

SISTER   Everything .
That boy was as clean as a whistle
And even he got cast as a gangster.
And now his brother's
Selling Mandy with his jeans round his ankles.
You give them everything.

BROTHER   'Them'? Who's 'them'?

SISTER   The system.

BROTHER   Are you for real?
'The system'?

SISTER   What do you think we're dealing with here?
We need people like you
God help me but we do
To turn up and represent.

BROTHER   I did.

SISTER   You left.

BROTHER   I didn't want to be there.

SISTER   *I* don't wanna be there.
            No one wants to be there.

BROTHER   So why you bothering?

SISTER   We're fighting.
            We're not giving up.

BROTHER   'We'? Who's 'we'?

SISTER   The community.

BROTHER   There is no community.
            There's just you, screaming into a microphone
            It's got nothing to do
            With justice
            It's a safety blanket, man.
            He's gone.
            And you can't move on.

SISTER   You think this is just about Brian?

BROTHER   What else is it about?

SISTER   Brian is every black man and black woman –

BROTHER   He's just Brian.
            He shouldn't have to be anyone else.
            I shouldn't have to care about anyone else.
            And I don't.

            [Pause]

SISTER   I don't want to hear from you ever again.

LOVER SAYS GOODBYE

[1st anniversary of Brian's death]

LOVER   Been a year Brian. A year.

Sold the flat.

The others'll be here in a bit.

We still talk.

They're nice to me.

I've met someone.

I'm happy.

He's kind.

He's a bit awkward actually.

He's not vain.

He doesn't try to control me.

He really loves me.

He's a photographer. Not a very good one. I tell
him he's great. He needs it.

Some people do.

He's white, Brian.

He's *ginger.*

He's less likely to get killed by the police.

That's important to me.

I'm not going to come here again.

Goodbye.

MOTHER/SON 4

[MOTHER is performing a ritual]

MOTHER   Yemoja, Blessed Mother of the Seas,
Let Your Sacred Waters wash over him
Mother, Embrace him, Cleanse him, Nurture
    him
Yemoja, Beautiful One
Who wears the Seven Skirts of the Seven Seas,
My Son
Buoy him, free him, grant him safe passage
from this terrible place
To where he belongs.
Please, I beg of you, find him a way
as you found a way here
for us.
I failed him.
I ripped him from his homeland in the hope of
something better
And they destroyed him.
My first born son.
If a way
Could be found
To bring him here
Can a way not be found to take him elsewhere
Where he might find peace to rest?

Custody

Please I beg of you
Do this for me.
I failed him once
I cannot fail him again.
My boy needs you.
I need you.
Please, most kind Yemoja
Grant him, I beg of you, safe passage.

[Silence]

SON   Mum.

MOTHER   Son.

SON   Hi Mum.

MOTHER   How are you?

SON   Seven Seven Seven

MOTHER   No.

SON   Bar Bar Bar

MOTHER   I SAID NO!

[Silence]

SON   Big Mac and fries

MOTHER   I do not wish to hear your
Whinings and bleatings.

You are a man
You were a man
And now you mewl like a kitten runt
You disgust me.
You have exhausted me.
I have prayed, made offerings,
I have pleaded with Elegbara
I have begged with Yemoja
I have torn my heart out and wrung it dry
And yet still you turn up tugging at my skirt
And I ask myself why?
Why you?
Why nobody else?
If you cannot pass through
It can only be there is something rotten in you.
You are cursed.
I disown you,
You are nothing to me
You may not return
I forbid it.
You may coast in your ocean of nothing for
     good
You are good for nothing
This is the proof of it.
A bad apple, son.
I thought it was your brother but no, you are
     the one
May the sharks devour you for I am done.
Begone.

[Silence]

MOTHER   Son –

SON   Cherry cherry cherry
                 Seven Seven
                 Bar Bar
                 Milk
                 Bananas, Bananas, Bananas, Bananas,
                 Watermelon, Horseshoe, Diamond, Pear
                 Big Win, Big Win [etc]

[MOTHER collapses and has a stroke. BROTHER enters and tends to her]

SISTER CAN'T DO IT

[SISTER is about to address a public meeting. Mic in hand]

SISTER   [To us] Here we go. One more time...

[Pause. She looks out at the crowd]

                 I'm tired, Brian.
                 Of this.
                 It's relentless.
                 When I get pumped up it's just muscle memory
                 A distant connect to when I really was angry
                 Year and a half I've been standing up here
                 Raising hell and bringing fire
                 And I am tired.
                 Know what I want, Brian?
                 I want to go shopping.
                 I want to moan about work.
                 Want to get a boyfriend.
                 Want to be boring.

I'm sorry, brother, I can't do it anymore.
Forgive me, I beg you
And let me go.

[SISTER walks off the stage. Her phone goes]

SISTER   What? Where?
            I'm coming.

HOSPITAL

[MOTHER is recovering from a stroke. BROTHER and SISTER by her bedside]

SISTER   You were right.

BROTHER   Excuse me?

SISTER   You were right
            About Brian.

[BROTHER gets his phone out]

SISTER   What you doing?

BROTHER   D'you mind repeating?
            I want to record this –
            Hard evidence

SISTER   Such a dick
            Sorry, Mum
            When are you gonna grow up?

Custody

BROTHER   When are you gonna chill out?
You need a man, girl.

SISTER   Yeah, tell me about it.
[Pause]
When you called I was about to do an event

BROTHER   How inconvenient.

SISTER   I couldn't do it.
I walked away.
I said I'm done, I'm finished
And the phone started ringing.

BROTHER   Done? Finished?
What you on about?

SISTER   I'm on about stopping,
Letting go
Like you said

BROTHER   I didn't say shit man –
Sorry Mum
You can't just walk away.

SISTER   Yes I can.

BROTHER   Nah, man.

SISTER   You said yourself –

BROTHER   I never said give up.

SISTER   But it's alright for you to do
            nothing?

BROTHER   I ain't got nothing to offer.
            But you got something special.
            There's people out there that really need you.

SISTER   What about what I need?

BROTHER   What about it?

SISTER   I can't do it.

BROTHER   Fuckin sell out
            Sorry Mum

SISTER   How dare you
            tell me that I'm a fuckin sell out
            Sorry Mum
            When you never do anything.
            I mean *anything*.
            You're a black hole, boy
            You suck in light
            And give nothing out.
            By the way I know what happened with his girl.

BROTHER   ...

SISTER   Nice touch brother
            Touch of class tapping that up.

BROTHER   Fuck you
            Sorry Mum

SISTER   Fuck you
          Sorry Mum

BROTHER   Fuck you
          Sorry Mum

SISTER   Fuck you –

[MOTHER protests to the best of her ability]

SISTER   Sorry Mum

BROTHER   Sorry Mum

[MOTHER, distressed, demands they make peace]

BROTHER   I'm sorry.

SISTER   I'm sorry.

[Pause]

BROTHER   This is so shit man.
          Sorry Mum.

[MOTHER makes a noise/gesture to the effect of 'please, spare me']

SISTER   It's *so* shit.
          Sorry Mum.

[Silence]

BROTHER   You ever feel... angry?
          With him?

SISTER   I feel angry with everyone
          You. Mum.
          I mean what's she done?

BROTHER   What have *I* done?

SISTER   You haven't done anything.

BROTHER   I'm playing.

[Pause]

SISTER   Playing. I wanna do more playing.
          Less fighting. Less raging.
          Less thinking. Less hating.
          More being. Just... being.

BROTHER   That's deep man.
          Just sayin.

SISTER   Don't take the piss.
           [Pause]
          Thank you.

BROTHER   For what?

SISTER   For saying I'm special.

BROTHER   Just the truth.

SISTER   You're special too.

BROTHER   Ssh.

SISTER   [Moved] I'm sorry little bro.
            I'm so so sorry.

BROTHER   I said hush,
            Man, you worry too much.

SISTER   I do.

BROTHER   Want a hug?

SISTER   Yeah. I do.

BROTHER   [To MOTHER] What about you?

[MOTHER makes a noise]

BROTHER   Take that as a yes.

[They all embrace]

ACT FOUR

CHANCE ENCOUNTER

[Six months later. BROTHER bumps into LOVER, who is with her newborn baby]

BROTHER   Nah.

LOVER   Hi.

BROTHER   Rah.

LOVER   You just gonna stare at me?

BROTHER   Starin at the baby.

LOVER   Never seen one before?

BROTHER   Of course.
           I just...

LOVER   What?

BROTHER   Beautiful.
           How are you?

LOVER   Tired.

BROTHER   No doubt.
           Are you alright?

LOVER   I'm alright.
           How are you?

[BROTHER smiles. Pause]

BROTHER   Where d'you go?

LOVER   Is that a serious question?

BROTHER   Yeah.

LOVER   Newham.

[Pause]

BROTHER   You know it's two years on Tuesday.

LOVER   Yes.
I know.

BROTHER   We're going to –

LOVER   When he went
It was me
he was closest to.
It was me he made love to
And slagged you lot off to.
It was me that he kissed and hugged and
Teased
Not you.
Me.
But when he died
All of a sudden your blood turned thicker than
our loving water
Ranks closed.
All I had was my secondary grief
The girlfriend
The fiancée
The other one.
She'll get over it – she'll move on.
Well, that is exactly what I've done.
And on Tuesday I will remember him

My way
On my terms.
Now please...

BROTHER   I was just going to say –

LOVER   What?

BROTHER   I'm speaking at a Black Lives Matter thing.
            On Tuesday.

LOVER   Thought that was more your sister's thing.

BROTHER   She burnt out

LOVER   No doubt.
            Well earned rest for her mouth.

BROTHER   Oi!

LOVER   What?

BROTHER   [Laughs] 'Rest for her mouth'
            [pause]
            Mum had a stroke.

LOVER   I'm sorry.
            When?

BROTHER   Six months ago.

LOVER   How's she doing?

BROTHER   ...

LOVER   I'm sorry.

BROTHER   Shit happens.
    Shit happened.

LOVER   Yeah it did.

[Pause]

BROTHER   Yeah, anyway,
    Tuesday
    Malcom X Centre
    I'm gonna talk about Brian.
    I'd like you to be there.

LOVER   I never had you down for the community vibe.

BROTHER   Me neither!
    And I didn't think I'd be Mum's full time carer...

LOVER   You look alright with it.
    And it with you.

BROTHER   Yeah?

LOVER   You always were a sweet boy.
    Underneath it all.

BROTHER   Hush...
    Make a black man blush.

LOVER   I'm going.

BROTHER   You coming?
             Tuesday.

LOVER   No.
             I don't know.
             I'll think about it.

BROTHER STEPS UP

[The following Tuesday. BROTHER is addressing a public meeting through a microphone. SISTER, MOTHER and LOVER, with baby, sit on the stage behind him]

BROTHER   This is my first time doing anything like this
             Public speaking.
             It used to be my sister who got involved –
             I'm sure you all know her so
             Go easy
             On me.
             She's a hard act to follow.

             I googled the word 'hope' last night. This is
             what I got...
             'A feeling of
             expectation and desire
             for a particular thing
             to happen.'

             My brother was killed in police custody two

years ago.
His name was Brian.
Behind me you've got the people he left
    behind:
His mother, his sister, and his former partner.

When the officer came to break the news
The expression he used was
'There was a bit of scuffle, and I'm sorry to say
he passed away.'
'Passed away.'
What d'you reckon to that bro?
Did you 'pass away'?
I don't think so.
See...
Old men snoring in their favourite armchair;
they pass away.
Our Great Aunt Nina,
all fifteen stone of her,
she passed away.
You?
You didn't pass away, you didn't die, you
weren't killed
unlawfully
You were murdered.

I still talk to him.
We all do.
Ain't nothing new – talking to the dead
But it takes on a different aspect
When the deceased
Is denied
The truth of how his life

Was extinguished.
I'm haunted by him.

I'll level with you
We didn't really get on once we were grown.
Don't look at me like that, bro!
I know what you think of me.
Smalltime, layabout wannabe thug –
And you're right.
He's right – I was.
But neither him nor me deserve to die in a
police cell surrounded by people who hate us.

These are hate crimes.

I'm not gonna talk about why this happens
And why we're watchin it on our phones every
    day
And why it will happen again and again
Because it will.
I don't want to talk about that

I wanna talk about how you handle it.

When you are denied justice,
Your grief is *arrested.*
You are stuck in it.
You're in limbo.
We're all in limbo.
Nothing we can do about that.
Nothing can change that.

Custody

So what's the point in us meeting up like this?
I used to think it was a waste of time
Sometimes I still do
It's February, it's cold
You're thinkin *really?*
Do I *have* to?

And if you want to go then go.
That's cool.
I'm not here for you –
I'm doin this for me.
It gives me an identity
A purpose
A focus.
If you're not feeling this then give yourself
a break.
You haven't given up the 'fight' –
This is coping.
This is hoping.

There is no solution to what we're going
    through.
There is no cure.
Rather, it's a paradox that we have to manage.

I didn't come up with that.
I heard it on the radio.

Find your hope.
Treasure it.
Protect it with your *life.*

Tom Wainwright

I didn't hear that on the radio.
That one right there?
That's mine.

Also available from Team Angelica Publishing

'Reasons to Live' by Rikki Beadle-Blair
'What I Learned Today' by Rikki Beadle-Blair

'Faggamuffin' by John R Gordon
'Colour Scheme' by John R Gordon
'Souljah' by John R Gordon

'Fairytales for Lost Children' by Diriye Osman

'Black & Gay in the UK – an anthology' edited by John R Gordon & Rikki Beadle-Blair

'More Than – the Person Behind the Label' edited by Gemma Van Pragh, John R Gordon & Rikki Beadle-Blair

'Tiny Pieces of Skull' by Roz Kaveney

'Slap' by Alexis Gregory

Fimí sílẹ̀ Forever by Nnanna Ikpo

Lightning Source UK Ltd.
Milton Keynes UK
UKOW05f1802230317
297379UK00001B/1/P